EXTRAORDINARY GOD

by G. Allen Jackson

The Foundation of an Extraordinary Life

Published by Intend Publishing
1921 New Salem Road, Hwy. 99
Murfreesboro, TN 37128

Special Sales:
Most Intend books are available
at special quantity discounts when
purchased in bulk by corporations,
organizations and special-interest
groups. Custom imprinting or excerpting
can also be done to fit special needs.
For more information, please
email contact@intendministries.org.

■ ■ ■ ■ TABLE OF CONTENTS

Contents

A man stood in the crowd one day watching Jesus handle an extended confrontation worse than the most intense and combative press conference you've ever heard. He was impressed with Jesus' answers, Mark tells us (Mark 12:28), so he asked Jesus an honest question: "Of all the commandments, which is the most important?" Which is a lot like the question we all ask God in one way or another: Lord, what do you expect from me? What should I really do? What's the bottom line, the central purpose—what's this life all about, Lord?

Most of us know how Jesus answered. We remember the Great Commandment: "Love the Lord your God with all your heart and with all your soul and with all your mind and with all your strength.' The second is this: 'Love your neighbor as yourself.' There is no commandment greater than these" (Mark 12:30-31). Except that isn't exactly what Jesus said. His answer began, "The most important one," answered Jesus, "is this: 'Hear, O Israel, the Lord our God, the Lord is one" (Mark 12:29). If we're carefully identifying commandments, the first one Jesus mentioned is "Hear!" As in listen, pay attention—"the Lord our God, the Lord is one!"

Before Jesus told us to love God, He pointed to the extraordinary God we are to love. Everything in the Christian life starts with God—who He is, what He does, what He has done for us. We love because He first loved us! And before we can make progress in loving God with all our hearts, all our souls, all our minds, and all our strength, we can get a lot of help by understanding this extraordinary God who is willing to love us and let us love Him back.

We're going to highlight parts of God's awesome character, use places in the Holy Land to illustrate that character, and learn together how to love this extraordinary God who loved us first. He demonstrated that love in this: that while we were yet sinners, Christ died for us! (see Romans 5:8). Our brief glimpses into God's character will include: Almighty God, God who is concerned, God who redeems, God who reveals, God who rewards, and God who requires. These are all facets of our extraordinary God, and yet when we are done, we will only have just begun our exploration.

Join us for these blessings.

Tools to Help You Have a Great Small Group Experience

Notice in the Table of Contents there are three sections:
1—Sessions (pg. 4) ;
2—Appendix (pg. 115); and
3—Small Group Leaders (pg. 123).
Familiarize yourself with the Appendix parts. Some of them will be used in the sessions themselves.

If you are facilitating/leading or co-leading a small group, the Small Group Leaders section on page 123 will give you some hard-learned experiences of others that will encourage you and help you avoid many common obstacles to effective small group leadership.

Use this workbook as a guide, not a straightjacket. If the group responds to the lesson in an unexpected but honest way, go with that. If you think of a better question than the next one in the lesson, ask it. Take to heart the insights included in the Frequently Asked Questions on page 117.

Enjoy your small group experience.

Read the Outline for Each Session on the next pages so that you understand how the sessions will flow.

Each session is divided into segments. The goal is to help the group interact with one another and the material presented. The Holy Spirit is our Teacher. As we open our hearts and lives, God will minister to us.

A typical group session for Extraordinary God will include the following:

STORY.

The lessons we learn during Extraordinary God are beautifully illustrated by the land of Israel, providing a glimpse of the way God has always and will always work in the world He has made. Each session will begin with a micro tour of a site in the land of Israel giving us an up close visit to where God continues to work out His plans and purposes.

GETTING STARTED.

The foundation for spiritual growth is an intimate connection with God and His family. A few people who really know you and who earn your trust provide a place to experience the life Jesus invites you to live. This section of each session typically offers you two options. You can get to know your whole group by using the icebreaker question(s), or you can check in with one or two group members—your spiritual partner(s)—for a deeper connection and encouragement in your spiritual journey.

DVD TEACHING SEGMENT.

Serving as a companion to the Extraordinary God small group discussion book is the Extraordinary God Video teaching. This DVD is designed to combine teaching segments from Pastor Allen Jackson along with a micro tour of Israel. Using the teaching video will add value to this 6-week commitment of doing life together and discovering how walking with Christ and understanding His Father changes everything.

DISCUSSION.

This section is where you will process as a group the teaching you heard and saw. The focus won't be on accumulating information but on how we should live in light of the Word of God. We want to help you apply the insights from Scripture practically, creatively, and from your heart as well as your head. At the end of the day, allowing the timeless truths from God's Word to transform our lives in Christ is our greatest aim.

APPLICATION.

We let the truth we are learning travel the 18 inches from our cranium (mind) to our cardium (heart, emotions, and will) in this portion. This is where the Bible instructs us to *"Do not merely listen to the word, and so deceive ourselves. Do what it says"* (James 1:22). Many people skip over this aspect of the Christian life because it's scary, relationally awkward, or simply too much work for their busy schedules. But Jesus wanted all of His disciples to help outsiders connect with Him, to know Him personally, and to carry out His commands. This doesn't necessarily mean preaching on street corners. It could mean welcoming a few newcomers into your group, hosting a short-term group in your home, or walking through this study with a friend. In this study, you'll have an opportunity to go beyond Bible study to biblical living.

GOING DEEPER.

If you have time and want to dig deeper into more Bible passages about the topic at hand, we've provided additional passages and questions. Your group may choose to do study homework ahead of each meeting in order to cover more biblical material. If you prefer not to do study homework, the Deeper Bible Study section will provide you with plenty to discuss within the group. These options allow individuals or the whole group to expand their study, while still accommodating those who can't do homework or are new to your group.

DAILY REFLECTIONS.

Each week on the Daily Devotionals pages we provide scriptures to read and reflect on between group meetings. We suggest you use this section to seek God on your own throughout the week. This time at home should begin and end with prayer. Don't get in a hurry; take enough time to hear God's direction.

WEEKLY MEMORY VERSES.

For each session we have provided a Memory Verse that emphasizes an important truth from the session. This is an optional exercise, but we believe that memorizing Scripture can be a vital part of filling our minds with God's will for our lives. We encourage you to give this important habit a try.

Caesarea Philippi/Jordan River

ALMIGHTY GOD

A. W. Tozer began his classic book entitled *Knowledge of the Holy* with this statement: "What comes into our minds when we think about God is the most important thing about us." Thinking about God on our own doesn't get us very far. In fact, if God didn't graciously and patiently reveal Himself to us by His Word, His Son, and His works, we wouldn't have a clue! But God loved us and graciously chose not to leave us clueless, letting us know all we need to know in order to respond to Him.

■ ■ ■ STORY - Dan/Lebanon

Both the city and the area called Dan in Israel have been the northern end of the land since the days of Joshua. Today these lands border Lebanon. When people wanted to speak of all Israel, north to south, they spoke of Dan to Beersheba. We will see in this session the evidence that Israel lives in a precarious situation between her enemies and the sea. And yet, as has always been the case, what ultimately matters in the life of Israel is not the size of her armed forces or the strength of her foes, but the fact that God has made Israel His people. Only what He allows to happen will happen to this land that He has declared is His own. The land of Israel is a living canvas displaying the power of an Almighty God to watch over His own.

Getting Started

We will begin with a question or brief activity designed to put us on the same page for the session. Since this is your first time together, take a few minutes to make sure everyone knows each other's names.

1. As we begin this new series, tell the rest of your group at least one trait or experience involving God that you would call extraordinary.

_____

_____

_____

_____

2. What places in the world (whether you've been to the Holy Land or not) most cause you to think about God?

_____

_____

_____

_____

EXTRAORDINARY GOD

dvd session 1

Throughout the sessions in *Extraordinary God* we're going to be hearing an encouraging introduction from several hosts, some pointed teaching from Pastor Allen Jackson, and some on location stories from Israel that highlight some aspect of the lesson for the session. With that possibility in mind, let's begin our teaching for this session:

Use the space below for notes, questions, or comments you want to bring up in the discussion later.

_____

_____

_____

_____

_____

_____

_____

_____

_____

_____

_____

_____

dvd **session 1**

A. We Serve an Extraordinary God

1 Samuel 2:2
There is no one holy like the LORD; there is no one besides you; there is no Rock like our God.

1. Hannah's prayer celebrates God's _____.

2. Worship is _____ for us.

3. God has provided _____ counsel.

4. There is only one _____ God.

B. Our God is Extraordinary

1. Israel _____ God's power.

2. _____ is one of the best demonstrations of God's power.

3. We belong to an _____ God too!

View into Lebanon

EXTRAORDINARY GOD

dvd **session 1**

C. God's Promises

Psalm 125:1-2; 4-5

¹ *Those who trust in the Lord are like Mount Zion, which cannot be shaken but endures forever.* ² *As the mountains surround Jerusalem, so the Lord surrounds his people both now and forevermore.* ⁴ *Do good, O Lord, to those who are good, to those who are upright in heart.* ⁵ *But those who turn to crooked ways the Lord will banish with the evildoers. Peace be upon Israel.*

1. God _____ over you and me today.

2. Those who trust in the Lord are like Mt. Zion, which cannot be shaken, but _____ forever.

3. We can have God's peace in the midst of _____.

Answer Key:
A- 1 (faithfulness); 2 (good); 3 (dependable); 4 (almighty)
B- 1 (demonstrates); 2 (protection); 3 (Extraordinary God)
C- 1 (watches); 2 (endures); 3 (conflict)

■ ■ ■ DISCUSSION

Using the questions that follow, we will review and expand on the teaching we just experienced.

God gave us, through Moses, the Ten Commandments. They have never been rescinded.

Read Exodus 20:1-17.

And God spoke all these words: ²"I am the LORD your God, who brought you out of Egypt, out of the land of slavery. ³You shall have no other gods before me. ⁴You shall not make for yourself an idol in the form of anything in heaven above or on the earth beneath or in the waters below. ⁵You shall not bow down to them or worship them; for I, the LORD your God, am a jealous God, punishing the children for the sin of the fathers to the third and fourth generation of those who hate me, ⁶ but showing love to a thousand [generations] of those who love me and keep my commandments. ⁷You shall not misuse the name of the LORD your God, for the LORD will not hold anyone guiltless who misuses his name. ⁸Remember the Sabbath day by keeping it holy. ⁹Six days you shall labor and do all your work, ¹⁰but the seventh day is a Sabbath to the LORD your God. On it you shall not do any work, neither you, nor your son or daughter, nor your manservant or maidservant, nor your animals, nor the alien within your gates. ¹¹For in six days the LORD made the heavens and the earth, the sea, and all that is in them, but he rested on the seventh day. Therefore the LORD blessed the Sabbath day and made it holy. ¹²Honor your father and your mother, so that you may live long in the land the LORD your God is giving you. ¹³You shall not murder. ¹⁴You shall not commit adultery. ¹⁵You shall not steal. ¹⁶You shall not give false testimony against your neighbor. ¹⁷You shall not covet your neighbor's house. You shall not covet your neighbor's wife, or his manservant or maidservant, his ox or donkey, or anything that belongs to your neighbor."

1 What is the first commandment?

_____

_____

_____

_____

_____

_____

_____

2 The first commandment is a protective revelation. We can avoid trial and error. God tells us He has no equal. Identify "false Gods" from the Israelites' journey.

_____

_____

_____

3 In contemporary life, think of some things we are warned to avoid because they are harmful; list three or four. Why do you suppose avoidance of harmful things is often difficult?

_____

_____

_____

"...and the king made two calves of gold... and he set one in Beth-el, and the other put he in Dan." (I Kings 12:28-29)

4 What is the epic story that introduces the entire Bible to us?

_____

_____

_____

Genesis 1:1-5

In the beginning God created the heavens and the earth. ²Now the earth was formless and empty, darkness was over the surface of the deep, and the Spirit of God was hovering over the waters. ³And God said, "Let there be light," and there was light. ⁴God saw that the light was good, and he separated the light from the darkness. ⁵God called the light "day," and the darkness he called "night." And there was evening, and there was morning--the first day.

5 If God is the Creator, what does that establish about His authority over all things?

_____

_____

_____

_____

_____

■ ■ ■ APPLICATION

Now it's time to make some personal applications to all we've been thinking about in the last few minutes.

6 Contemporary "false gods" are often less recognizable. Anything or anyone we trust for our well-being before Almighty God is a false god. List three or four false gods from your life experience.

_____

_____

7 God has watched over the people of Israel for more than three millennia. In the land and scattered throughout the nations, God has been faithful to them. Identify three or four ways God intervened for the Israelites.

_____

_____

8 As Christ followers, we too are the people of God. He is our Extraordinary God!

_____

_____

Read 1 Peter 2:9-10
⁹But you are a chosen people, a royal priesthood, a holy nation, a people belonging to God, that you may declare the praises of him who called you out of darkness into his wonderful light. ¹⁰Once you were not a people, but now you are the people of God; once you had not received mercy, but now you have received mercy.

9 Share an experience when God has intervened on your behalf.

_____

_____

_____

_____

_____

_____

_____

10 The Israelites struggled to remain obedient. So do we. What things contribute to our tendency to compromise and be inconsistent?

_____

_____

11 How does modern Israel remind you that God is both faithful and powerful?

_____

_____

12 Trust in the Lord is the antidote to fear. What fears confront you today?

_____

_____

_____

Read Psalm 125:1-5
Those who trust in the LORD are like Mount Zion, which cannot be shaken but endures forever. ²As the mountains surround Jerusalem, so the LORD surrounds his people both now and forevermore. ³The scepter of the wicked will not remain over the land allotted to the righteous, for then the righteous might use their hands to do evil. ⁴Do good, O LORD, to those who are good, to those who are upright in heart. ⁵But those who turn to crooked ways the LORD will banish with the evildoers. Peace be upon Israel.

13 Discuss what a "trust response" would look like.

_____

_____

_____

PRAYER REQUESTS:

_____

_____

_____

Close the session in prayer. Pray for others in the group. Use the following prayer as you lean into God:

Heavenly Father,
We acknowledge You as the creator and sustainer of all things. As we begin these weeks together we ask that You would direct our time together. Give us listening ears and receptive hearts to the message You have for us. Deliver us from anything that separates us from Your best for our lives. May we have the wisdom and humility to choose You and turn away from destructive things. Almighty God we need Your help: You are our God and Our Redeemer. Amen.

NOTES

_____
_____
_____
_____
_____
_____
_____
_____
_____
_____
_____
_____
_____
_____
_____
_____
_____
_____
_____
_____
_____
_____
_____
_____
_____
_____
_____
_____

GOING DEEPER - PERSONAL DEVOTION & REFLECTION

You can explore the following Bible passages behind the teaching for this session as a group (if there is time) or on your own between sessions.

Read 1 Samuel 2:1–10.
Pastor Allen described this prayer as one of his favorite passages of Scripture because this thankful woman took time to express in great detail not only her gratefulness, but also her understanding of exactly Who she was grateful to. He noted that the prayer is life changing for us if we can find space for it in our hearts.

In 1 Samuel 1:11, Hannah made the following promise to God in prayer: *"O LORD Almighty, if you will only look upon your servant's misery and remember me, and not forget your servant but give her a son, then I will give him to the LORD for all the days of his life, and no razor will ever be used on his head."*

- What promises have you made and what things have you given to God? How has that worked out for you?

- If you only had 1 Samuel 2:1–10 to go on, what would you know about God Almighty?

- How does Hannah (particularly in verse 2) demonstrate the incomparable aspects of the Lord God Almighty?

Read Psalm 125:1–5.

This is one of fifteen Psalms in this section that are called in Jewish tradition the Songs of Ascent. These Psalms were used by pilgrims each year when they made the journey to Jerusalem for the Passover. The phrases were on their minds as they walked up the rising land on which the City of David rested among the mountains.

- What symbols (like mountains) do you think about when you are meditating on Almighty God's trustworthiness? What two characteristics of Mt. Zion does the writer highlight for confidence?

_____

_____

_____

_____

_____

_____

_____

_____

_____

This Psalm, like many, contrasts the main two kinds of human life.

- What kind of profile for the righteous and the wicked could you compile from these verses? On what basis do you put yourself in either of those groups?

_____

_____

_____

_____

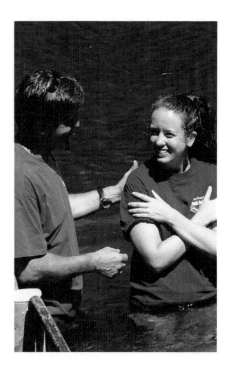

Note in Hebrews 12:18–29 how the writer uses the mountain and shaking ideas to illustrate the security we have in Jesus.

- How does Psalm 125 help you understand Hebrews 12:28, Therefore, since we are receiving a kingdom that cannot be shaken, let us be thankful, and so worship God acceptably with reverence and awe, for our "God is a consuming fire"?

Entrance Gate to City of Dan from days of Abraham

Bible verses to help you
reflect upon and apply the
insights from this session.

Day 1
Psalm 73:25 | Desiring the Extraordinary God

Whom have I in heaven but you? And earth has nothing I desire besides you.

Reflection Question:
How high does God rank on the list of things you desire?

_____

_____

_____

Day 2
Zechariah 4:6 | Extraordinary Power

So he said to me, "This is the word of the LORD to Zerubbabel: 'Not by might nor by power, but by my Spirit,' says the LORD Almighty."

Reflection Question:
Where do we find strength to live the Christian life?

_____

_____

_____

_____

_____

Day 3
Isaiah 6:1–3 | Worrying Alone

¹In the year that King Uzziah died, I saw the Lord seated on a throne, high and exalted, and the train of his robe filled the temple. ²Above him were seraphs, each with six wings: With two wings they covered their faces, with two they covered their feet, and with two they were flying. ³And they were calling to one another: "Holy, holy, holy is the LORD Almighty; the whole earth is full of his glory."

Reflection Question:
What is it about God that causes you to want to worship Him?

_____

_____

_____

Day 4
Psalm 125:1 | Trustworthy

Those who trust in the LORD are like Mount Zion, which cannot be shaken but endures forever.

Reflection Question:
What makes you want to trust in a God who is Almighty?

_____

_____

_____

Day 5
Genesis 17:1-2 | Almighty Faithfulness

¹When Abram was ninety-nine years old, the LORD appeared to him and said, "I am God Almighty; walk before me and be blameless. ² Then I will make my covenant between me and you and will greatly increase your numbers."

Reflection Question:
What specific promises has God made to you that you are counting on for a lifetime and beyond?

_____

_____

_____

_____

_____

_____

_____

_____

_____

_____

_____

_____

Weekly Memory Verse

Those who trust in the LORD are like Mount Zion, which cannot be shaken but endures forever. Psalm 125:1

David's Citidel, Old City in Jerusalem

GOD IS CONCERNED

Welcome to week two of *Extraordinary God!* This time we will travel into Jerusalem and think about the ways God has watched over that ancient city. One of our temptations when we catch a glimpse of the majesty, holiness, and power of God is that we can't imagine that He would care for us. David wrote in Psalm 8:3-4, *"When I consider your heavens, the work of your fingers, the moon and the stars, which you have set in place, what is man that you are mindful of him, the son of man that you care for him?"* We see in Jerusalem, and throughout God's Word, the concern God has for each of us. Jesus said, *"Look at the birds of the air; they do not sow or reap or store away in barns, and yet your heavenly Father feeds them. Are you not much more valuable than they?"* Matthew 6:26. We can gain this same perspective as we look at David's city and God's faithfulness through the centuries.

■ ■ ■ STORY - Jerusalem

The ancient, the old, and the new stand side-by-side in Jerusalem. There are sights to see everywhere, and more to see underground, where the layers of the city are revealed. First mentioned in the Bible in Genesis 14:17–24 as Salem, the city in which Melchizedek was king and a priest of the one God and where Abraham went to pay tithes after his victory over the raiders who kidnapped his nephew, Lot. The city's special role is mentioned in 1 Kings 14:21, "Jerusalem, the city the LORD had chosen out of all the tribes of Israel in which to put his Name."

Jerusalem is also mentioned in the last two chapters of the Bible: "I saw the Holy City, the new Jerusalem, coming down out of heaven from God, prepared as a bride beautifully dressed for her husband. And I heard a loud voice from the throne saying, 'Now the dwelling of God is with men, and he will live with them. They will be his people, and God himself will be with them and be their God'" (Revelation 21:2–3).

Getting Started

We will begin with a question or brief activity designed to put us on the same page for the session. Continue to make sure everyone knows each other's names.

1 As an opener, talk to one another about what you know or have heard about Jerusalem. Perhaps one or more people in the group have visited the city. What was your most indelible memory of the experience?

_____

_____

_____

2 As a benefit for those who might be joining us for the first time this session, what insight from last week would you be willing to share with the rest of the group?

_____

_____

_____

dvd **session** 2

Throughout the sessions in *Extraordinary God* we're going to be hearing an encouraging introduction from several hosts, some pointed teaching from Pastor Allen Jackson, and some on location stories from Israel that highlight some aspect of the lesson for the session. With that possibility in mind, let's begin our teaching for this session:

Video Lesson
G. ALLEN JACKSON
INTENDRESOURCES.CO

EXTRAORDINARYGOD
THE FOUNDATION OF AN EXTRAORDINARY LIFE

Use the space below for notes, questions, or comments you want to bring up in the discussion later.

_____

_____

_____

_____

_____

_____

_____

_____

_____

_____

_____

_____

_____

_____

dvd **session 2**

A. God has Chosen Jerusalem as His own

(2 Chronicles 6: 6)
I have chosen Jerusalem for my Name to be there, and I have chosen David to rule my people Israel.

1. Being chosen by God does not remove us from _____.

2. God cares for Jerusalem and God cares for _____.

B. The God Who Cares for Jerusalem Cares for You and Me!

(Isaiah 59:1)
Surely the arm of the LORD is not too short to save, nor his ear too dull to hear.
1. Our God is _____.

2. Walk toward God in a _____ way.

3. God will see His purposes emerge in the midst of _____ circumstances.

Dome of the Rock on Temple Mount

dvd **session 2**

C. The Heart of Our Extraordinary God

(Matthew 6:26)
Look at the birds of the air; they do not sow or reap or store away in barns, and yet your heavenly Father feeds them. Are you not much more valuable than they?

   1. You are _____ to God.

   2 . Not perfect.

   3. Not always consistent.

   3. Nevertheless, valuable to God.

D. Extraordinary God— Merciful in His Concern

(Isaiah 1:18-19)
[18]*"Come now, let us reason together, says the LORD: though your sins are like scarlet, they shall be as white as snow; though they are red like crimson, they shall become like wool."* [19]*If you are willing and obedient, you will eat the best from the land;*

   1. He knows the _____ and intents of our hearts.

   2. God is _____ in His concern for us.

■ ■ ■ DISCUSSION

Using the questions that follow, we will review and expand on the teaching we just experienced.

1 God has chosen Jerusalem as His own, a unique city for His special purposes. Of all the places in the world, where will Jesus return?

_____

_____

_____

_____

_____

2 Pastor Allen talked about Jerusalem being conquered 28 times. Being chosen does not remove us from the realm of difficulty. Discuss some of the difficulties Jerusalem faces today.

_____

_____

_____

_____

Read Matthew 6:26.
"Look at the birds of the air; they do not sow or reap or store away in barns, and yet your heavenly Father feeds them. Are you not much more valuable than they?"

3 When we feel inadequate or unworthy of God's best, Jesus assures us in this verse that God cares for us because of His faithfulness, not ours. Share a time when God intervened for you.

_____

_____

_____

4 What actions do you take when you feel concerned for something or someone?

_____

_____

_____

_____

_____

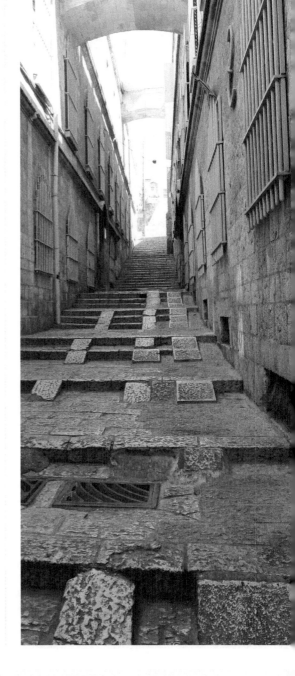

■ ■ ■ APPLICATION

Now it's time to make some personal applications to all we've been thinking about in the last few minutes.

5 Have you experienced a life circumstance or difficulty that made you feel disqualified from being chosen by God?

_____

_____

_____

_____

6 Discuss ideas from your experiences that have added momentum to your God journey.

_____

_____

_____

_____

_____

_____

_____

Church of St. Anne at Pool of Bethesda

EXTRAORDINARY GOD

Read Isaiah 1:19.
If you are willing and obedient, you will eat the good things of the land;

7 Being chosen comes with responsibility. What is required of us?

_____

_____

_____

_____

8 What is the difference in willingness and obedience? Which do you need more of today?

_____

_____

_____

9 As you have matured spiritually, describe how you have learned new responsibilities.

_____

_____

_____

_____

_____

_____

Use the following prayer to end the session:

Heavenly Father,
Thank you for opening my heart and mind to the truth of your word. I pray for the Church today, that we would be awakened to the purposes of God for this generation. We choose to humble ourselves and turn to you in re-pentance --asking for your mercy upon our nation. We pray for the peace of Jerusalem. Through our lives may your purposes be accomplished and the name of Jesus lifted up. Amen.

NOTES

_____

_____

_____

_____

_____

_____

_____

_____

_____

_____

_____

_____

_____

_____

_____

_____

_____

_____

_____

_____

_____

_____

_____

NOTES

You can explore the following Bible passages behind the teaching for this session as a group (if there is time) or on your own between sessions.

Read Isaiah 62:1–12.

As a prophet called by God, Isaiah had many hard things as well as hopeful things to say about Jerusalem. On God's behalf he pronounced judgment and forgiveness, disaster and restoration to the city and its inhabitants. This chapter offers a glimpse of Jerusalem's ultimate restoration. God is in relationship with us as He is with Jerusalem, with eternity in mind.

- Based on verses 1–5 how would you describe God's feelings about Jerusalem?

_____

_____

_____

- What instruction do we find in verses 6–7 about our attitude toward Jerusalem?

_____

_____

_____

Western Wall,
Old City Jerusalem

- How do verses 8–12 indicate a global role for Jerusalem in God's plans?

_____

_____

_____

_____

- What sense do you get about God's promises to you based on the way He keeps His word to Jerusalem?

_____

_____

_____

NOTES

DAILY REFLECTIONS

Bible verses to help you reflect upon and apply the insights from this session.

■ ■ ■ DAILY REFLECTIONS

Daily Reflections

Day 1
1 Peter 5:7 | Offloading anxiety
Cast all your anxiety on him because he cares for you.

Reflection Question:
What are some anxieties you can "cast" on Him today?

_____

_____

_____

_____

Day 2

Matthew 6:26 | A Lesson from Birds
Look at the birds of the air; they do not sow or reap or store away in barns, and yet your heavenly Father feeds them. Are you not much more valuable than they?

Reflection Question:
Besides the birds you might see today, what other reminders do you have of God's value over your life?

_____

_____

_____

_____

_____

Day 3
John 10:11–13 | Deep Concern
[11] *I am the good shepherd. The good shepherd lays down his life for the sheep. [12] The hired hand is not the shepherd who owns the sheep. So when he sees the wolf coming, he abandons the sheep and runs away. Then the wolf attacks the flock and scatters it. [13] The man runs away because he is a hired hand and cares nothing for the sheep.*

Reflection Question:
How does God's concern get personal for you? In what ways have you experienced Jesus as your good shepherd?

_____

_____

_____

EXTRAORDINARY GOD

Day 4
Matthew 23:37-39 | Jesus and Jerusalem
³⁷O Jerusalem, Jerusalem, you who kill the prophets and stone those sent to you, how often I have longed to gather your children together, as a hen gathers her chicks under her wings, but you were not willing. ³⁸Look, your house is left to you desolate. ³⁹For I tell you, you will not see me again until you say, "Blessed is he who comes in the name of the Lord."

Reflection Question:
In what ways could you apply these words of sorrow and concern by Jesus for Jerusalem to your own life?

_____

_____

_____

Day 5
Isaiah 59:1 | God's Abilities and Attentiveness
Surely the arm of the LORD is not too short to save, nor his ear too dull to hear.

Reflection Question:
In what ways has God demonstrated His concern over your life?

_____

_____

_____

Weekly Memory Verse

Look at the birds of the air; they do not sow or reap or store away in barns, and yet your heavenly Father feeds them. Are you not much more valuable than they?
(Matthew 6:26)

Jezreel Valley

GOD REDEEMS

One way to describe the Bible is two chapters of Creation followed by the rest of Genesis and 65 more books on Redemption. The fall of humanity that occurs in Genesis 3 has deeply affected the entirety of human history, right down to today. God is still in the redeeming business, and each of us needs to experience the work that only He can do in our lives.

■ ■ ■ STORY - Mt. Carmel

When we imagine Mt. Carmel, we often think about confrontation and observation. From its heights we can look over the vast rolling plain between the mountains and the Mediterranean ocean. At our feet is the open ground of the Jezreel Valley and Har Meggido, or what we now call Armageddon, the place of the final armed conflict. Israel was challenged by God to stop compromising. They had included Baal worship in their religious activity. The lesson of Mt. Carmel is God's intolerance for compromise because it is so destructive to His people.

Getting Started

We will begin with a question or brief activity designed to put us on the same page for the session. Continue to make sure everyone knows each other's names.

1 High school, college, or professional, what championship game/contest have you witnessed that left the greatest impression on you? Why?

_____

_____

_____

2 As a benefit to those who might be joining us for the first time, what insight from last week would you be willing to share with the group?

_____

_____

_____

_____

_____

EXTRAORDINARY GOD

dvd session 3

Throughout the sessions in *Extraordinary God* we're hearing some pointed teaching from Pastor Allen Jackson as well as some video visits to sites in the Holy Land. The places and events that have occurred in the Promised Land can serve as powerful reminders of the way God deals with us. With that possibility in mind, let's begin our teaching for this session:

Use the space provided below for any notes, questions, or comments you want to bring up in the discussion later.

_____

_____

_____

_____

_____

_____

_____

_____

_____

_____

_____

_____

dvd **session 3**

A. God Redeems

(1 Kings 18:20–21)
20So Ahab sent word throughout all Israel and assembled the prophets on Mount Carmel. 21Elijah went before the people and said, "How long will you waver between two opinions? If the LORD is God, follow him; but if Baal is God, follow him." But the people said nothing.

1. God _____ this confrontation.

2. God _____Elijah.

3. The people said _____.

4. God _____ displayed His power.

B. The Power of God

(Colossians 2:13–15)
13When you were dead in your sins and in the uncircumcision of your sinful nature, God made you alive with Christ. He forgave us all our sins, 14having canceled the written code, with its regulations, that was against us and that stood opposed to us; he took it away, nailing it to the cross. 15And having disarmed the powers and authorities, he made a public spectacle of them, triumphing over them by the cross.

1. God _____ out to us.

2. God _____ us even when we are disobedient.

3. God _____ for us when we are unfaithful to Him.

dvd session 3

C. Ultimate Reality

(Titus 3:5)
He saved us, not because of righteous things we had done, but because of his mercy. He saved us through the washing of rebirth and renewal by the Holy Spirit,

1. Being good is not _____.

2 . We are a people_____.

3. Our God is_____!

Jezreel Valley

Answer Key:
A – 1 (initiated); 2 (prepared); 3 (nothing); 4 (still)
B – 1 (reaches); 2 (loves); 3 (cares)
C – 1 (adequate); 2 (redeemed); 3 (Extraordinary)

■ ■ ■ DISCUSSION

Using the questions that follow, we will review and expand on the teaching we just experienced.

(1 Kings 18:19)
Now summon the people from all over Israel to meet me on Mount Carmel. And bring the four hundred and fifty prophets of Baal and the four hundred prophets of Asherah, who eat at Jezebel's table.

1 How many false prophets did King Ahab gather (Baal and Asherah) to join him on Mt. Carmel?

_____

_____

_____

_____

_____

_____

_____

_____

2 Imagine the scene, King Ahab and all his false prophets gathered on one side. In opposition stood Elijah. How do you suppose he felt?

_____

_____

_____

_____

_____

ISRAEL

Road Map

With compliments

Sar-El Tours

LEBANON

SYRIA

3 Elijah offered the people a new beginning. How did they respond?

(1 Kings 18:27)
At noon Elijah began to taunt them. "Shout louder!" he said. "Surely he is a god! Perhaps he is deep in thought, or busy, or traveling. Maybe he is sleeping and must be awakened."

4 How did Elijah treat the prophets of Baal and Asherah as they prepared their sacrifice?

_____

_____

_____

_____

_____

_____

_____

_____

_____

_____

_____

SURREXIT ELIAS
PROPHETA QUASI
IGNIS ET VERBUM
IPSIUS QUASI FACULA
ARDEBAT

ו قام ايليا النبى كنار وكلامكلام
كالمشعل

ויקם אליהו הנביא כאש
ודברו כלפיד בער

Elijah on Mt. Carmel

■ ■ ■ APPLICATION

Now it's time to make some personal applications to all we've been thinking about in the last few minutes.

5 Describe a circumstance when you had to take a stand for godliness.

_____

_____

_____

_____

6 The Israelites did not reject God; they had fallen prey to compromise. In what ways do we struggle with compromise?

_____

_____

_____

_____

_____

_____

7 The Israelites refused to answer Elijah when he asked a question, however after the supernatural involvement of God, they repented. Discuss a time you broke free of compromise.

_____

_____

_____

(Colossians 2:13-15)
[13]When you were dead in your sins and in the uncircumcision of your flesh, God made you alive with Christ. He forgave us all our sins, [14]having canceled the charge of our legal indebtedness, which stood against us and condemned us; he has taken it away, nailing it to the cross. [15]And having disarmed the powers and authorities, he made a public spectacle of them, triumphing over them by the cross.

_____

_____

_____

_____

8 How has God demonstrated a supernatural power to deliver us?

_____

_____

_____

9 In His love, God demonstrates His power to redeem His people. Describe a time you witnessed or experienced God's deliverance.

_____

_____

_____

10 God used Elijah as an important tool to bring deliverance to the people. Discuss people God has used to initiate freedom in your life.

_____

_____

_____

_____

_____

_____

_____

_____

Close the session in prayer. Pray for others in the group. Use the prayer below for your personal response to this session:

Heavenly Father,
I give you glory and honor for calling me out of darkness into the Kingdom of Your Son. You have redeemed my life from futility and frustration. I want to cooperate with You and Your invitations towards righteousness, holiness and purity. Holy Spirit open my mind to the truth of a living God. May the character of Jesus grow within me. I thank you that whatever stands before me, you are my redeemer. Your strength is sufficient, Your resources are abundant and Your grace is extended. In Jesus' name, Amen.

NOTES

EXTRAORDINARY GOD

NOTES

GOING DEEPER - PERSONAL DEVOTION & REFLECTION

You can explore the following Bible passages behind the teaching for this session as a group (if there is time) or on your own between sessions.

Read Colossians 2:6–15.
As he did in many of his letters, the Apostle Paul explained to the Colossians the process of salvation and sanctification, how God finds us lost and in sin, and makes us citizens of the kingdom of His Son, Jesus. This passage is filled with pictures of God's work in our lives.

- How do verses 6–7 summarize the Christian life for you?

_____

_____

_____

_____

_____

_____

_____

_____

- In verses 8–12 Paul contrasts what we have in Christ with the "hollow and deceptive philosophy" the world continues to offer us. How are these two "ways" radically different?

_____

_____

_____

_____

- Verses 13–15 include not only a picture of our condition apart from Christ but a description of what Jesus did to settle matters once for all on our behalf. Identify all the specific actions Jesus undertook in enduring the cross.

_____

_____

_____

EXTRAORDINARY GOD

Read Isaiah 43:1–3.

Much like Elijah, the prophet Isaiah was instructed by God to issue some of the harshest indictments against the Chosen People as well as some incomparable soaring words of hope, not only for Israel but for all people. Isaiah informs us that our righteousness is like filthy rags and then announces that One is coming who will be called Wonderful Counselor, Prince of Peace. Unless we understand our condition, we can't appreciate to what lengths God went to redeem us.

- In verse 1, what reasons does God give to Israel for telling them not to fear?

_____

_____

_____

_____

_____

_____

_____

_____

_____

- How would such assurances affect you?

_____

_____

_____

_____

- Verses 2–3 contain two water passages and one fire passage. What do all these have in common when it comes to facing or avoiding these matters in our lives?

_____

_____

_____

NOTES

_____

_____

_____

_____

_____

_____

_____

_____

_____

_____

_____

_____

_____

_____

_____

_____

_____

_____

_____

_____

■ ■ ■ DAILY REFLECTIONS

■ ■ ■ ■ ■ ■

Bible verses to help you
reflect upon and apply the
insights from this session.

■ ■ ■ DAILY REFLECTIONS

Day 1
Isaiah 43:2-3 | Desiring an Extraordinary God

²When you pass through the waters, I will be with you; and when you pass through the rivers, they will not sweep over you. When you walk through the fire, you will not be burned; the flames will not set you ablaze. ³For I am the LORD, your God, the Holy One of Israel, your Savior; I give Egypt for your ransom, Cush and Seba in your stead.

Reflection Question:
What challenges in your life are most like water that could drown you or flames that could burn you? What has God promised here?

_____

_____

_____

_____

Day 2
Colossians 2:13 | Dead; then Alive

When you were dead in your sins and in the uncircumcision of your sinful nature, God made you alive with Christ. He forgave us all our sins.

Reflection Question:
In what ways have you experienced what it means to be alive in Christ?

_____

_____

_____

_____

_____

_____

_____

Jezreel Valley

Day 3
2 Corinthians 7:10 | The Pain of Redemption
Godly sorrow brings repentance that leads to salvation and leaves no regret, but worldly sorrow brings death.

Reflection Question:
When has God allowed you to go through difficult times until you arrived at repentance?

_____

_____

_____

_____

Day 4
Romans 5:8 | Redeeming Love Demonstrated
But God demonstrates his own love for us in this: While we were still sinners, Christ died for us.

Reflection Question:
What makes you most certain of God's love for you? Why?

_____

_____

_____

_____

_____

_____

Day 5
Titus 3:5 | Never on Our Own
He saved us, not because of righteous things we had done, but because of his mercy. He saved us through the washing of rebirth and renewal by the Holy Spirit

Reflection Question:
How does renewal come to our lives?

_____

_____

_____

_____

Weekly Memory Verse

When you were dead in your sins and in the uncircumcision of your sinful nature, God made you alive with Christ. He forgave us all our sins. (Colossians 2:13)

Sea of Galilee

GOD REVEALS

By this session we should be settling into a level of comfort with the group, continuing to welcome any newcomers. During our time together we'll be taking a look at the way revelation always starts with God. We never discover anything about Him on our own. We don't catch God by surprise or find something He wanted to keep hidden. God is eager to let us know Him and find out enough about Him to keep us engaged for a lifetime—and eternity!

■ ■ ■ STORY - Galilee

Our backdrop for this session will be the Sea of Galilee, the large, fresh water lake that interrupts the Jordan River in its flow from northern Israel to the Dead Sea. As Pastor Allen will point out, sailing in a boat on the Sea of Galilee is like sitting in a panoramic theatre where every direction you look presents the scene of a Bible story. Jesus spent more time on and around the lake than anywhere else during His ministry. It would be fair to say that when God revealed Himself perfectly in Jesus, He did so with the Sea of Galilee in the background.

Getting Started

We will begin with a question or brief activity designed to put us on the same page for the session. Continue to make sure everyone knows each other's names.

1 What is your favorite story about Jesus around Galilee?

_____

_____

_____

2 The disciples were witnesses to many miracles. Share with the group a miracle you've witnessed.

_____

_____

_____

_____

_____

_____

_____

dvd session 4

Throughout the sessions in *Extraordinary God* we're hearing some pointed teaching from Pastor Allen Jackson as well as some video visits to sites in the Holy Land. The places and events that have occurred in the Promised Land can serve as powerful reminders of the way God deals with us. With that possibility in mind, let's begin our teaching for this session:

Use the space provided below for any notes, questions, or comments you want to bring up in the discussion later.

_____

_____

_____

_____

_____

_____

_____

_____

_____

_____

_____

_____

dvd **session 4**

A. God reveals Himself to people in every generation.

1. Jesus began His public _____ in Capernaum.

2. Some of the places around the Sea of Galilee that are sites of Jesus' ministry are:

   _____

   _____

   _____

B. Jesus has not changed.

1. We need to be _____ to the Truth about God.

C. Jesus has not changed.

(Hebrews 13:8)
Jesus Christ is the same yesterday and today and forever.

dvd **session 4**

D. The Holy Spirit is present to help us.

(John 14:26–27)

²⁶ But the Counselor, the Holy Spirit, whom the Father will send in my name, will teach you all things and will remind you of everything I have said to you. ²⁷Peace I leave with you; my peace I give you. I do not give to you as the world gives. Do not let your hearts be troubled and do not be afraid.

1. The Holy Spirit will not _____ you.

2. The Holy Spirit will teach us all_____.

E. Jesus' Revelation

(John 8:32)

Then you will know the truth, and the truth will set you free.

1. Freedom requires _____.

F. Jesus said, "Believe in Me."

1. The objective of having the truth of God revealed to you is to set free in us _____ in Jesus.

Answer Key:
A – (ministry)
B – (awakened)
D – 1 (dominate); 2 (Truth)
E – (growth)
F – (new belief)

■ ■ ■ DISCUSSION

Using the questions that follow, we will review and expand on the teaching we just experienced.

Read Matthew 8:25-29.

25The disciples went and woke him, saying, "Lord, save us! We're going to drown!" 26He replied, "You of little faith, why are you so afraid?" Then he got up and rebuked the winds and the waves, and it was completely calm. 27The men were amazed and asked, "What kind of man is this? Even the winds and the waves obey him!" 28When he arrived at the other side in the region of the Gadarenes, two demon-possessed men coming from the tombs met him. They were so violent that no one could pass that way. 29"What do you want with us, Son of God?" they shouted. "Have you come here to torture us before the appointed time?"

1　List some of the differing revelations the disciples experienced as they got to know Jesus.

_____

_____

_____

_____

_____

2　How did the disciples respond to what they were experiencing with Jesus?

_____

_____

_____

_____

_____

_____

_____

_____

_____

_____

_____

Read Mark 7:17-19

^{17}After he had left the crowd and entered the house, his disciples asked him about this parable. ^{18}"Are you so dull?" he asked. "Don't you see that nothing that enters a person from the outside can defile them? ^{19}For it doesn't go into their heart but into their stomach, and then out of the body."

Read Matthew 4:18-20

^{18}As Jesus was walking beside the Sea of Galilee, he saw two brothers, Simon called Peter and his brother Andrew. They were casting a net into the lake, for they were fishermen. ^{19}"Come, follow me," Jesus said, "and I will send you out to fish for people." ^{20}At once they left their nets and followed him.

3 On a scale of 1-10, how were the disciples doing at understanding what was being put before them?

_____

_____

_____

_____

4 What is the necessary first step of discipleship?

_____

_____

_____

_____

Boat on the Sea of Galilee

■ ■ ■ APPLICATION

Now it's time to make some personal applications to all we've been thinking about in the last few minutes.

5 The disciples were observant Jews. They had religious holidays, went to synagogue, and kept religious rules, yet they had much to learn about the Kingdom of God. To varying degrees we are religious yet with much to learn. Share something you have learned about Jesus or the Kingdom of God in recent weeks.

Read John 14:26-27
²⁶But the Counselor, the Holy Spirit, whom the Father will send in my name, will teach you all things and will remind you of everything I have said to you. ²⁷Peace I leave with you; my peace I give you. I do not give to you as the world gives. Do not let your hearts be troubled and do not be afraid.

6 We have a Helper. What two things will the Holy Spirit do for us?

_____

_____

_____

_____

_____

7 The disciples learned about Jesus in the midst of struggles, storms, sick family members, and responsibility to feed large numbers with little money. We have life challenges that hold potential for a life revelation of Jesus. What aspect of Jesus' life would you like revealed? Explain.

_____

_____

_____

_____

_____

8 The disciples struggled to understand and believe; so will we. What has helped you to overcome doubt and fear about following Jesus?

_____

_____

_____

_____

_____

Read John 8:32

Then you will know the truth, and the truth will set you free.

9 Truth brings freedom. Bondage persists when Truth is absent. Describe a time when God's Truth brought freedom to your life.

_____

_____

_____

_____

_____

_____

PRAYER REQUESTS:

_____

_____

_____

_____

_____

_____

_____

_____

Pray for others in the group. Use the following prayer as you lean into God:

Heavenly Father, thank You for sending Jesus, a living revelation. I pray today that You would bring to my life a revelation of Jesus. Help me to know Him as Lord of all. Holy Spirit, open my eyes to the wonder of redemption. May the power of the cross be unveiled to me as never before. I yield my life and strength for the purposes of the Kingdom of God. Through my life may the name of Jesus be exalted. Amen.

NOTES

EXTRAORDINARY GOD

NOTES

_____

_____

_____

_____

_____

_____

_____

_____

_____

_____

_____

_____

_____

_____

_____

_____

_____

_____

_____

_____

_____

_____

_____

_____

You can explore the following Bible passages behind the teaching for this session as a group (if there is time) or on your own between sessions.

Read John 14:15–27; 16:7–15. Twice during the Apostle John's extended account of the Last Supper (John 13–17), he includes sections of Jesus' teaching about the Holy Spirit and His ministry in the world. Part of it has to do with the Holy Spirit's work in our lives as believers and part of it highlights His work in us even before we're believers.

- What do verses 14:16–17 spell out about the Holy Spirit and His specific work for and in us?

_____

_____

_____

_____

_____

_____

_____

- How does Jesus weave the roles of the Father, the Holy Spirit, and Himself together in these verses? In what ways do we experience God's presence?

_____

_____

_____

_____

- Read verses 14:25–27. List the things the Holy Spirit will bring to your life.

_____

_____

_____

- In 16:7–11, what three specific roles does Jesus say the Holy Spirit will pursue in the world?

_____

_____

_____

_____

_____

_____

_____

- In what ways is the Holy Spirit a significant part of God's revelation of Himself to us?

_____

_____

_____

_____

_____

_____

_____

NOTES

Bible verses to help you reflect upon and apply the insights from this session.

DAILY REFLECTIONS

Day 1
Hebrews 13:8 | God Unchanging
Jesus Christ is the same yesterday and today and forever.

Reflection Question:
What do you find most challenging or comforting about the unchanging nature of Jesus?

_____

_____

_____

Day 2
John 1:14 | Grace and Truth
The Word became flesh and made his dwelling among us. We have seen his glory, the glory of the One and Only Son, who came from the Father, full of grace and truth.

Reflection Question:
Why is Jesus the ultimate revelation of God in the world?

_____

_____

_____

_____

_____

Day 3
John 14:26-27 | The Counselor Who Is Peace
26But the Counselor, the Holy Spirit, whom the Father will send in my name, will teach you all things and will remind you of everything I have said to you. 27Peace I leave with you; my peace I give you. I do not give to you as the world gives. Do not let your hearts be troubled and do not be afraid.

Reflection Question:
In what way would you connect the presence of the Holy Spirit and the reality of peace in your life?

_____

_____

_____

Day 4
John 8:32 | Freedom
Then you will know the truth, and the truth will set you free

Reflection Question:
What truth was Jesus referring to that is our ultimate access to freedom?

_____

_____

_____

_____

Day 5

John 14:11 | Believe

Believe me when I say that I am in the Father and the Father is in me; or at least believe on the evidence of the works themselves.

Reflection Question:

How has the Holy Spirit revealed Christ to you and led you to believe in Him?

_____

_____

_____

_____

_____

_____

_____

Weekly Memory Verse

^{26}But the Counselor, the Holy Spirit, whom the Father will send in my name, will teach you all things and will remind you of everything I have said to you. ^{27}Peace I leave with you; my peace I give you. I do not give to you as the world gives. Do not let your hearts be troubled and do not be afraid.
(John 14:26-27)

Roman Theater, Beth Shan

GOD REWARDS

There is always a tension between God's grace and our self-awareness. Clearly we never earn God's mercy and blessings. Yet a great freedom comes when we are awakened to a life God rewards.

The realization that God responds to those who seek Him opens doors of faith and hope. If you want God's best, give God your best.

STORY - Beth Shan

The city of Beth Shan is the gateway to the Jezreel Valley. A strategic location and a consistent water source made it a thriving city for 1000 years before Jesus. In Jesus' days, Beth Shan (Scythopolis) was a thriving Roman city.

Getting Started

We will begin with a question or brief activity designed to put us on the same page for the session. Continue to make sure everyone knows each other's names.

1 What is a favorite city that you have visited?

_____

_____

_____

_____

_____

_____

2 Describe an unexpected gift you've received.

_____

_____

_____

_____

_____

_____

_____

_____

dvd **session 5**

Throughout the sessions in *Extraordinary God* we're hearing some pointed teaching from Pastor Allen Jackson as well as some video visits to sites in the Holy Land. The places and events that have occurred in the Promised Land can serve as powerful reminders of the way God deals with us. With that possibility in mind, let's begin our teaching for this session:

Video Lesson
G. ALLEN JACKSON
INTENDRESOURCES.CC

EXTRAORDINARYGOD
THE FOUNDATION OF AN EXTRAORDINARY LIFE

Use the space below for notes, questions, or comments you want to bring up in the discussion later.

---

dvd **session 5**

A. God Rewards

1. Beth Shan was God's _____ 2000 years later.

2. God _____ for His people.

3. God is a _____ of His people.

(1 Kings 3:10-13)
[10]The Lord was pleased that Solomon had asked for this. [11]So God said to him, "Since you have asked for this and not for long life or wealth for yourself, nor have asked for the death of your enemies but for discernment in administering justice, [12]I will do what you have asked. I will give you a wise and discerning heart, so that there will never have been anyone like you, nor will there ever be. [13]Moreover, I will give you what you have not asked for—both wealth and honor— so that in your lifetime you will have no equal among kings.

B. God Requires

(Luke 18:22)
When Jesus heard this, he said to him, "You still lack one thing. Sell everything you have and give to the poor, and you will have treasure in heaven. Then come, follow me."

1. That young man could not imagine a reward for following Jesus that was greater than the things he _____ had.

2. There's a reward for _____ the Lord.

Answer Key:
A – 1 (reward); 2 (provides); 3 (rewarder)
B – 1 (already); 2 (following)

Roman Theater

■ ■ ■ DISCUSSION

Using the questions that follow, we will review and expand on the teaching we just experienced.

Read Deuteronomy 28:1-2.
¹ If you fully obey the Lord your God and carefully follow all his commands I give you today, the Lord your God will set you high above all the nations on earth. ²All these blessings will come on you and accompany you if you obey the Lord your God:

1 What two things are required of those who seek the Lord?

_____

_____

_____

_____

_____

_____

_____

_____

_____

2 God responds to our choices with what two specific promises about His blessings? "They will come upon you and...

_____

_____

_____

Read Hebrews 11:6.
And without faith it is impossible to please God, because anyone who comes to him must believe that he exists and that he rewards those who earnestly seek him.

3 Without faith it is impossible to please God. The desire to please God is essential. What can you do that pleases God? What can you do that displeases God?

_____

_____

_____

_____

_____

4 What is the current trend of your life?

_____

_____

_____

_____

_____

_____

■ ■ ■ APPLICATION

Now it's time to make some personal applications to all we've been thinking about in the last few minutes.

Read Mark 10:17-22.

17 As Jesus started on his way, a man ran up to him and fell on his knees before him. "Good teacher," he asked, "what must I do to inherit eternal life?" 18 "Why do you call me good?" Jesus answered. "No one is good— except God alone. 19 You know the commandments: 'You shall not murder, you shall not commit adultery, you shall not steal, you shall not give false testimony, you shall not defraud, honor your father and mother.'" 20 "Teacher," he declared, "all these I have kept since I was a boy." 21 Jesus looked at him and loved him. "One thing you lack," he said. "Go, sell everything you have and give to the poor, and you will have treasure in heaven. Then come, follow me." 22 At this the man's face fell. He went away sad, because he had great wealth.

5 How does Mark say Jesus felt about this young man? It's important to remember God loves us even when we are reluctant followers.

_____

_____

6 This young man's obedience resulted in an invitation from Jesus. What was the invitation?

_____

_____

7 He declined Jesus' invitation because he could not imagine a reward for following Jesus any greater than the things he already had. Describe a time you struggled with an invitation from the Lord because the reward seemed obscure.

_____

_____

EXTRAORDINARY GOD

8 Beth Shan was buried for 2000 years. Sometimes God's reward is not apparent. Describe a time when you were surprised by the benefit of cooperating with God

_____

_____

9 Take a moment to share one thing that has been significant to you so far in this study.

_____

_____

_____

_____

_____

_____

_____

Close the session in prayer. Pray for others in the group. Use the following prayer as you lean into God:

Thank you for watching over my life. Your grace and mercy have provided opportunities and liberty to me. Open my eyes to your presence and purposes as never before. I choose to cooperate with you, to yield to you in my thoughts, attitudes and actions. I put my trust in you as my deliverer. Forgive me for ignoring you and for my persistent rebellion. I turn to you in repentance. I give you glory and honor as Lord and King of my life. In Jesus' name, Amen.

NOTES

_____

_____

_____

_____

_____

_____

_____

_____

_____

_____

_____

_____

_____

_____

_____

_____

_____

_____

_____

_____

_____

_____

_____

_____

NOTES

You can explore the following Bible passages behind the teaching for this session as a group (if there is time) or on your own between sessions.

Read Luke 18:18–30.
The encounter between Jesus and the rich young ruler is most often used as an example of how easy it is to be held captive by the things of this world instead of placing our faith in Christ.

- What did the man actually ask Jesus? What's the difference between "earning" and "inheriting"? How does it affect your understanding of access to eternal life?

_____

_____

_____

_____

_____

_____

_____

- Why do you think Jesus responded with "Why do you call me good? No one is good--except God alone" before He continued with His answer?

_____

_____

- Jesus could have challenged the man's response ("All these I have kept since I was a boy"), but He didn't. Why not? (see vs. 24–25).

_____

_____

- In what ways do verses 26–30 preserve the doctrine of salvation by grace while teaching the reality of immediate and eternal rewards for faithfulness?

Read Matthew 25:14–30.

Jesus delivered His parable of the talents during the final days of His life here. It's easy to get sidetracked regarding the identity of the talents and not take time to think about the results Jesus described. When we use our "talents" faithfully, what can we expect? The point of this parable is not to shame those who are faithless but to encourage us to realize God gives each of us a specific set of circumstances and resources through which He can work.

• Why do you think Jesus includes three different servants with three different trust packages? (Look particularly at vs. 15).

_____

_____

_____

• In verses 21 and 23, how does the master respond to the good report from his faithful servants?

_____

_____

_____

• Why didn't the master accept the explanation of the third servant in vs. 24–28?

_____

_____

_____

• What encouragement and warning was Jesus telling all of us in vs. 29–30?

_____

_____

_____

NOTES

DAILY REFLECTIONS

Bible verses to help you reflect upon and apply the insights from this session.

Day 1
Psalm 27:13 | Enduring for Good

I am still confident of this: I will see the goodness of the LORD in the land of the living.

Reflection Question:
How is seeing the goodness of the Lord a reward in your life?

_____

_____

_____

Day 2
Hebrews 11:6 | Promised Rewards

And without faith it is impossible to please God, because anyone who comes to him must believe that he exists and that he rewards those who earnestly seek him.

Reflection Question:
In what ways would you describe your desires for God as earnest?

_____

_____

_____

_____

Day 3
Luke 18:29–30 | Now and Later

[29]"I tell you the truth," Jesus said to them, "no one who has left home or wife or brothers or parents or children for the sake of the kingdom of God [30]will fail to receive many times as much in this age and, in the age to come, eternal life."

Reflection Question:
What did Jesus mean by "left" in this statement? In what ways have you seen the reality of rewards in this age, and anticipate those in the age to come?

_____

_____

_____

Day 4
Matthew 6:1–2 | Deferring Rewards

Be careful not to do your 'acts of righteousness' before men, to be seen by them. If you do, you will have no reward from your Father in heaven. [2]So when you give to the needy, do not announce it with trumpets, as the hypocrites do in the synagogues and on the streets, to be honored by men. I tell you the truth, they have received their reward in full.

Reflection Question:
How are you doing in the 'random and anonymous acts of kindness' that only God knows about?

_____

_____

_____

Day 5
Hebrews 11:26 | Moses' Rewards
He regarded disgrace for the sake of Christ as of greater value than the treasures of Egypt, because he was looking ahead to his reward.

Reflection Question:
Who are your examples of people who have held the rewards of this life lightly because they are/were looking to a greater reward with Christ?

_____

_____

_____

_____

_____

_____

Weekly Memory Verse

And without faith it is impossible to please God, because anyone who comes to him must believe that he exists and that he rewards those who earnestly seek him.
(Hebrews 11:6)

Dead Sea

SESSION SIX
GOD REQUIRES

As we conclude our study of Extraordinary God, it is helpful to remember that in His great love for us He requires a response. Our relationship with God is strengthened as we realize we have the privilege of responding to Him.

The Dead Sea lies at the bottom of the rift valley. In Roman days, the salt mined from the area was payment for Roman legions. Today, the Israelites harvest minerals of great value from the sea. For centuries, the Dead Sea has generated wealth but never supported life—it is far too salty. It is a powerful reminder that our lives consist of far more than wealth.

Getting Started

We will begin with a question or brief activity designed to put us on the same page for the session. Continue to make sure everyone knows each other's names.

1 What have you discovered during these sessions of Extraordinary God that you believe will make a difference in your life going forward?

_____

_____

_____

2 Given the experience we've had in these sessions, what are some other topics or questions you would like to see our small group address at some point in the future?

_____

_____

_____

_____

_____

dvd **session 6**

Throughout the sessions in *Extraordinary God* we're hearing some pointed teaching from Pastor Allen Jackson as well as some video visits to sites in the Holy Land. The places and events that have occurred in the Promised Land can serve as powerful reminders of the way God deals with us. With that possibility in mind, let's begin our teaching for this session:

Use the space below for any notes, questions, or comments you want to bring up in the discussion later.

_____

_____

_____

_____

_____

_____

_____

_____

_____

_____

_____

_____

_____

dvd **session 6**

A. God has Requirements for His people

(Deuteronomy 10:12)
And now, O Israel, what does the LORD your God ask [or require] of you but to fear the LORD your God, to walk in all his ways, to love him, to serve the LORD your God with all your heart and with all your soul,

1. When we're birthed in the Kingdom of God, we receive mercy, grace, and _____.

B. Our Response

(Luke 6:37-38)
[37]*"Do not judge, and you will not be judged. Do not condemn, and you will not be condemned. Forgive, and you will be forgiven.* [38]*Give, and it will be given to you. A good measure, pressed down, shaken together and running over, will be poured into your lap. For with the measure you use, it will be measured to you."*

1. When we _____ with God, an extraordinary life is possible for us.

Answer Key:
A – (forgiveness)
B – (cooperate)
C – 1 (retain); 2 (expects)

dvd **session 6**

C. Our Contribution

Acts 7:53 (NASB)
you who received the law as ordained by angels, and yet did not keep it.

   1. They chose not to _____ it.

   2. God _____ something of His people.

■ ■ ■ DISCUSSION

Using the questions that follow, we will review and expand on the teaching we just experienced.

1 Recognizing God's mercy and grace towards us is often challenging in the midst of life's pressures. Take a moment and discuss some of God's blessings in your life.

_____

_____

_____

_____

Read Deuteronomy 10:12.
And now, Israel, what does the Lord your God ask of you but to fear the Lord your God, to walk in obedience to him, to love him, to serve the Lord your God with all your heart and with all your soul,

2 What four things does this passage tell us God requires of us?

_____

_____

_____

_____

3 God asks (or requires) something of His people. Describe how God's requirements affect your daily life.

_____

_____

_____

_____

_____

_____

_____

EXTRAORDINARY GOD

4 Pastor Allen said as we grow up in the Lord there are some responsibilities we should accept in response to God. Discuss some of the responsibilities you have accepted as a maturing child of God.

_____

_____

_____

_____

_____

5 In the past week, have you had a greater focus on pleasing God or God pleasing you?

_____

_____

_____

_____

_____

_____

_____

_____

At this point we move in our discussion from talking about implications of the teaching to application of the teaching. If we grasp what the idea means we can talk about what it means in our lives.

Read Luke 6:37-38.

³⁷ Do not judge, and you will not be judged. Do not condemn, and you will not be condemned. Forgive, and you will be forgiven. ³⁸Give, and it will be given to you. A good measure, pressed down, shaken together and running over, will be poured into your lap. For with the measure you use, it will be measured to you."

6 "Give, and it will be given to you." There is a correlation between giving and what is given to you. From the following list: mercy, forgiveness, time, and money—which is easiest for you to give? Explain.

_____

_____

_____

_____

_____

7 From the same list, which do you prefer to rescue? Explain.

_____

_____

_____

_____

_____

_____

_____

_____

8   Using the biblical principle of sowing and reaping, what behavior would bring mercy toward you: forgiveness: time: money?

_____

_____

9   God will be no one's debtor. Describe a time you gave of yourself to the Lord and experienced His response.

_____

_____

10   Before you go, take a moment to discuss the next steps for your group—celebration dinner, commitment to pray for one another, attend church together, participate in another study, etc.

_____

_____

_____

_____

PRAYER REQUESTS:

_____

_____

_____

_____

_____

_____

_____

Close the session in prayer. Pray for others in the group. Use the following prayer to commit yourself to a life learning not to worry:

Thank You for pouring out blessings and provision upon my life. I choose to respond to You in obedience. My delight is in yielding to my God and my Savior. Grant me a willing spirit and a listening ear. Teach us to encourage one another as we grow and mature. Help us to stand together in such a way that others might know Jesus Christ as Lord. May the name of Jesus be held in great esteem and honored through our actions. We rejoice in Your faithfulness to Your people. We rest today in the shadow of Your great strength. In Jesus' name, Amen.

NOTES

NOTES

GOING DEEPER - PERSONAL DEVOTION & REFLECTION

You can explore the following Bible passages behind the teaching for this session as a group (if there is time) or on your own between sessions.

Read Mark 12:28–34.
In one of the central events of Scripture, Jesus was asked to state the most important requirement from God. He didn't hesitate. And the questioner immediately affirmed what He said. Ultimately, the question isn't about knowing what God requires but whether or not we are willing to accept His willingness to help us do what He requires.

- Why did the scribe ask Jesus his question? How did he respond to Jesus' answer?

_____

_____

- In Jesus' answer what is the first actionable/applicable verb? (Hint: it isn't love)

_____

_____

_____

- Jesus echoes the means of expressing love for God that were originally recorded in Deuteronomy 6:1-9. List some specific actions that might fit in each of those categories. For example, how do you love God with your whole mind?

_____

_____

- The second part of the great commandment comes from Leviticus 19:18. Review Leviticus 19:9–18 and describe how Jesus' reference reflects a summary of what God requires from our horizontal relationships.

_____

_____

_____

_____

- Despite their agreement on the contents of God's expectations, why do you think Jesus told the man, "You are not far from the Kingdom of God"?

_____

_____

Read Micah 6:6–8.
In this passage, the prophet is meditating on his relationship with God and in particular the requirements the relationship includes. As has been repeatedly stated in the lesson, the reality of the requirements has nothing to do with earning a relationship with God; they have everything to do with expressing our response to the privilege of that relationship.

- What possible requirements does the prophet reject as ultimately inappropriate expressions of authentic response to God?

_____

_____

_____

In verse 8, in what ways can requirements be equated with good, as Micah does?

_____

_____

_____

Take a few minutes and brainstorm specific expressions of each of the following three required responses to God:
Doing justice…
Loving kindness…
Walking humbly with your God…

_____

_____

_____

_____

_____

_____

_____

_____

_____

_____

NOTES

_____
_____
_____
_____
_____
_____
_____
_____
_____
_____
_____
_____
_____
_____
_____
_____
_____
_____
_____
_____
_____

DAILY REFLECTIONS

Bible verses to help you
reflect upon and apply the
insights from this session.

DAILY REFLECTIONS

Day 1
Micah 6:8 | The Essential Requirements

He has showed you, O man, what is good. And what does the LORD require of you? To act justly and to love mercy and to walk humbly with your God.

Reflection Question:
Which of these requirements would you say God wants to see more apparent in your life?

_____

_____

_____

_____

Day 2
Deuteronomy 10:12–13 | For Our Good

¹² And now, O Israel, what does the LORD your God ask of you but to fear the LORD your God, to walk in all his ways, to love him, to serve the LORD your God with all your heart and with all your soul, ¹³and to observe the LORD's commands and decrees that I am giving you today for your own good?

Reflection Question:
As you consider those verbs: fear, walk, love, serve, and observe, which ones most cause you to ask God for help? Why?

_____

_____

Day 3
Hebrews 5:12–14 | Mature Diet

¹² In fact, though by this time you ought to be teachers, you need someone to teach you the elementary truths of God's word all over again. You need milk, not solid food! ¹³Anyone who lives on milk, being still an infant, is not acquainted with the teaching about righteousness. ¹⁴But solid food is for the mature, who by constant use have trained themselves to distinguish good from evil.

Reflection Question:
What does your current spiritual nourishment say about your level of maturity?

_____

_____

_____

_____

_____

Day 4

Luke 6:37–38 | Equal Measures

*37 Do not judge, and you will not
be judged. Do not condemn,
and you will not be condemned.
Forgive, and you will be forgiven.
38Give, and it will be given to you.
A good measure, pressed down,
shaken together and running over,
will be poured into your lap. For
with the measure you use, it will
be measured to you.*

Reflection Question:

How have you recently applied
the principle of treating others
exactly the way you long to be
treated?

_____

_____

_____

Day 5

Acts 7:51–53 | The Edge of Requirement

*51You stiff-necked people, with
uncircumcised hearts and ears!
You are just like your fathers:
You always resist the Holy Spirit!
52Was there ever a prophet your
fathers did not persecute? They
even killed those who predicted
the coming of the Righteous One.
And now 53you have betrayed and
murdered him-- you who have
received the law that was put into
effect through angels but have not
obeyed it.*

Reflection Question:

In what ways are you going
about keeping or obeying what
you know God desires from
your life?

_____

_____

_____

_____

Weekly Memory Verse

*12And now, O Israel, what
does the LORD your God
ask of you but to fear the
LORD your God, to walk
in all his ways, to love him,
to serve the LORD your
God with all your heart and
with all your soul, 13and
to observe the LORD's
commands and decrees
that I am giving you today
for your own good?*
(Deuteronomy 10:12–13)

APPENDIX

Great resources to help make your small group experience even better!

Appendix

What do we do on the first night of our group?

Like all fun things in life–have a party! A "get to know you" coffee, dinner, or dessert is a great way to launch a new study. You may want to review the Group Agreement (page 119) and share the names of a few friends you can invite to join you. But most importantly, have fun before your study time begins.

Where do we find new members for our group?

We encourage you to pray with your group and then brainstorm a list of people from work,

church, your neighborhood, your children's school, family, the gym, and so forth. Then have each group member invite several of the people on his or her list. No matter how you find participants, it's vital that you stay on the lookout for new people to join your group. All groups tend to go through healthy attrition–the result of moves, releasing new leaders, ministry opportunities, and so forth–and if the group gets too small, it could be at risk of shutting down. If you and your group stay open, you'll be amazed at the people God sends your way. The next person just might become a friend for life. You never know!

How long will this group meet?

It's totally up to the group–once you come to the end of this 6-week study. Most groups meet weekly for at least their first 6 weeks, but every other week can work as well.

At the end of this study, each group member may decide if he or she wants to continue on for another 6-week study. Some groups launch relationships for years to come, and others are stepping-stones into another group experience. Either way, enjoy the journey.

What if this group is not working for us?

You're not alone! This could be the result of a personality conflict, life stage difference, geographical distance, level of spiritual maturity, or any number of things. Relax. Pray for God's direction, and at the end of this 6-week study, decide whether to continue with this group or find another. You don't buy the first car you look at or marry the first person you date, and the same goes with a group. Don't bail out before the 6 weeks are up–God might have something to teach you. Also, don't run from conflict or prejudge people before you have given them a chance. God is still working in you too!

How do we handle the child care needs in our group?

We suggest that you empower the group to openly brainstorm solutions. You may try one option that works for a while and then adjust over time. Our favorite approach is for adults to meet in the living room or dining room, and to share the cost of a babysitter (or two) who can be with the kids in a different part of the house. In this way, parents don't have to be away from their children all evening when their children are too young to be left at home. A second option is to use one home for the kids and a second home (close by or a phone call away) for the adults. A third idea is to rotate the responsibility of providing a lesson or care for the children either in the same home or in another home nearby. This can be an incredible blessing for kids. Finally, the most common idea is to decide that you need to have a night to invest in your spiritual lives individually or as a couple, and to make your own arrangements for child care. No matter what decision the group makes, the best approach is to dialogue openly about both the problem and the solution.

OUR PURPOSE

To provide a predictable environment where participants experience authentic community and spiritual growth.

OUR PURPOSE

Group Attendance	To give priority to the group meeting. We will call or email if we will be late or absent. (Completing the Group Calendar on page 120 will minimize this issue.)
Safe Environment	To help create a safe place where people can be heard and feel loved. (Please, no quick answers, snap judgments, or simple fixes.)
Respect Differences	To be gentle and gracious to people with different spiritual maturity, personal opinions, temperaments, or "imperfections" in fellow group members. We are all works in progress.
Confidentiality	To keep everything shared strictly confidential and within the group, and to avoid sharing improper information about those outside the group.
Encouragement	To be not just takers but givers of life. We want to spiritually multiply our life by serving others with our God-given gifts.
Shared Ownership	To remember that every member is a minister and to ensure that each attender will share a small responsibility over time.

OUR EXPECTATIONS

- Refreshments _____
- Childcare _____
- When we will meet (day of week) _____
- Where we will meet (place) _____
- We will begin at (time) _____ and end at _____
- We will do our best to have some or all of us attend a worship service together. Our primary worship service time will be _____
- Date of this agreement _____
- Date we will review this agreement again _____
- Who (other than the leader) will review this agreement at the end of this study

  _____

SMALL GROUP CALENDAR

At the end of each meeting, review this calendar. Be sure to include birthdays, socials, church events, holidays, and mission/ministry projects. Go to intendresources.com for an electronic copy of this form and more.

Date	Lesson	Host Home	Refreshments	Leader
Monday, January 15	1	Bill	Joe	Bill

MEMORY VERSES

Session 1
*Those who trust in the LORD are like Mount Zion, which cannot be shaken but endures forever.
(Psalm 125:1)*

Session 2
Look at the birds of the air; they do not sow or reap or store away in barns, and yet your heavenly Father feeds them. Are you not much more valuable than they? (Matthew 6:26)

Session 3
*When you were dead in your sins and in the uncircumcision of your sinful nature, God made you alive with Christ. He forgave us all our sins.
(Colossians 2:13)*

Session 4
26But the Counselor, the Holy Spirit, whom the Father will send in my name, will teach you all things and will remind you of everything I have said to you. 27Peace I leave with you; my peace I give you. I do not give to you as the world gives. Do not let your hearts be troubled and do not be afraid. (John 14:26-27)

Session 5
And without faith it is impossible to please God, because anyone who comes to him must believe that he exists and that he rewards those who earnestly seek him. (Hebrews 11:6)

Session 6
*12And now, O Israel, what does the LORD your God ask of you but to fear the LORD your God, to walk in all his ways, to love him, to serve the LORD your God with all your heart and with all your soul, 13and to observe the LORD's commands and decrees that I am giving you today for your own good?
(Deuteronomy 10:12–13)*

PRAYER REQUESTS	PRAISE REPORTS
SESSION 1	
SESSION 2	
SESSION 3	
SESSION 4	
SESSION 5	
SESSION 6	

Appendix

SMALL GROUP LEADERS

Key resources to help your leadership experience be the best it can be.

If you're starting a new group, try planning an "open house" before your first formal group meeting. Even if you only have two to four core members, it's a great way to break the ice and to consider prayerfully who else might be open to join you over the next few weeks. You can also use this kick-off meeting to hand out study guides, spend some time getting to know each other, discuss each person's expectations for the group and briefly pray for each other.

A simple meal or good desserts always make a kick-off meeting more fun. After people introduce themselves and share how they ended up being at the meeting (you can play a game to see who has the wildest story!), have everyone respond to a few icebreaker questions: "What is your favorite family vacation?" or "What is one thing you love about your church/our community?" or "What are three things about your life growing up that most people here

don't know?" Next, ask everyone to tell what he or she hopes to get out of the study. You might want to review the Small Group Agreement and talk about each person's expectations and priorities. Finally, set an open chair (maybe two) in the center of your group and explain that it represents someone who would enjoy or benefit from this group but who isn't here yet. Ask people to pray about whom they could invite to join the group over the next few weeks. Hand out postcards and have everyone write an invitation or two. Don't worry about ending up with too many people; you can always have one discussion circle in the living room and another in the dining room after you watch the lesson. Each group could then report prayer requests and progress at the end of the session. You can skip this kick-off meeting if your time is limited, but you'll experience a huge benefit if you take the time to connect with each other in this way.

- **Sweaty palms are a healthy sign.** The Bible says God is gracious to the humble. Remember who is in control; if you feel inadequate, that is probably a good sign. Those who are soft in heart (and sweaty palmed) are those whom God is sure to speak through.

- **Seek support.** Ask your leader, co-leader, or close friend to pray for you and prepare with you before the session. Walking through the study will help you anticipate potentially difficult questions and discussion topics.

- **Bring your uniqueness to the study.** Lean into who you are and how God wants you to uniquely lead the study.

- **Prepare. Prepare. Prepare.** Go through the session several times. If you are using the DVD, listen to the teaching segment and choose the questions you want to be sure to discuss.

- **Ask for feedback so you can grow.** Perhaps in an email or on cards handed out at the study, have everyone write down three things you did well and one thing you could improve on. Don't get defensive, but show an openness to learn and grow.

- **Prayerfully consider launching a new group.** This doesn't need to happen overnight, but God's heart is for this to happen over time. Not all Christians are called to be leaders or teachers, but we are all called to be "shepherds" of a few someday.

- **Share with your group what God is doing in your heart.** God is searching for those whose hearts are fully His. Share your trials and victories. We promise that people will relate.

- **Congratulations!** You have responded to the call to help shepherd Jesus' flock. There are a few other tasks in the family of God that surpass the contribution you will be making. As you prepare to lead, whether it is one session or the entire series, here are a few thoughts to keep in mind. We encourage you to read these and review them with each new discussion leader before he or she leads.

- **Remember that you are not alone.** God knows everything about you, and He knew that you would be asked to lead your group. Remember that it is common for all good leaders to feel that they are not ready to lead. Moses, Solomon, Jeremiah and Timothy - they all were reluctant to lead. God promises, "Never will I leave you; never will I forsake you" (Hebrews 13:5). Whether you are leading for one evening, for several weeks, or for a lifetime, you will be blessed as you serve.

- **Don't try to do it alone.** Pray right now for God to help you build a healthy leadership team. If you can enlist a co-leader to help you lead the group, you will find your experience to be much richer. This is your chance to involve as many people as you can in building a healthy group. All you have to do is call and ask people to help, you'll be surprised at the response.

- **Just be yourself.** If you won't be you, who will? God wants you to use your unique gifts and temperament. Don't try to do things exactly like another leader; do them in a way that fits you! Just admit it when you don't have an answer, and apologize when you make a mistake. Your group will love you for it, and you'll sleep better at night!

- **Prepare for your meeting ahead of time.** Review the session and the leader's notes, and write down your responses to each question. Pay special attention to exercises that ask group members to do something other than engage in discussion. These exercises will help your group live what the Bible teaches, not just talk about it. Be sure you understand how an exercise works, and bring any necessary supplies (such as paper and pens) to your meeting. If the exercise employs one of the items in the appendix, be sure to look over that item so you'll know how it works. Finally, review "Outline for Each Session" so you'll remember the purpose of each section in the study.

- **Pray for your group members by name.** Before you begin your session, go around the room in your mind and pray for each member by name. You may want to review the prayer list at least once a week. Ask God to use your time together to touch the heart of every person uniquely. Expect God to lead you to whomever He wants you to encourage or challenge in a special way. If you listen, God will surely lead!

- **When you ask a question, be patient.** Someone will eventually respond. Sometimes people need a moment or two of silence to think about the question, and if silence doesn't bother you, it won't bother anyone else. After someone responds, affirm the response with a simple "thanks" or "good job." Then ask, "How about somebody else?" or "Would someone who hasn't shared like to add anything?" Be sensitive to new people or reluctant members who aren't ready to say, pray or do anything. If you give them a safe setting, they will blossom over time.

- **Provide transitions between questions.** When guiding the discussion, always read aloud the transitional paragraphs and the questions. Ask the group if anyone would like to read the paragraph or Bible passage. Don't call on anyone, but ask for a volunteer, and then be patient until someone begins. Be sure to thank the person who reads aloud.

- **Break up into small groups each week, or they won't stay.** If your group has more than seven people, we strongly encourage you to have the group gather sometimes in discussion circles of three or four people during the SHARING TOGETHER sections of the study. With a greater opportunity to talk in a small circle, people will connect more with the study, apply more quickly what they're learning and ultimately get more out of it. A small circle also encourages a quiet person to participate and tends to minimize the effects of a more vocal or dominant member. It can also help people feel more loved in your group. When you gather again at the end of the section, you can have one person summarize the highlights from each circle. Small circles are also helpful during prayer time. People who are unaccustomed to praying aloud will feel more comfortable trying it with just two or three others. Also, prayer requests won't take as much time, so circles will have more time to actually pray. When you gather back with the whole group, you can have one person from each circle briefly update everyone on the prayer requests. People are more willing to pray in small circles if they know that the whole group will hear all the prayer requests.

- **One final challenge (for new or first time leaders):**
Before your first opportunity to lead, look up each of the five passages listed below. Read each one as a devotional exercise to help equip yourself with a shepherd's heart. Trust us on this one. If you do this, you will be more than ready for your first meeting.

Matthew 9:36
1 Peter 5:2-4
Psalm 23
Ezekiel 34:11-16
1 Thessalonians 2:7-8, 11-12

ABOUT THE AUTHOR

God is in the business of taking the ordinary and making it extraordinary. Pastor G. Allen Jackson is an excellent example of what God can do when people yield their lives to God. Growing up in rural Tennessee, Pastor Jackson literally worked in a barn while growing up around his father's equine veterinary practice.

G. Allen Jackson has worked with the congregation of World Outreach Church in Murfreesboro, Tennessee since 1981, serving as senior pastor for 25 years.

Under his leadership and vision, World Outreach Church fellowship has grown from 150 to 10,000. In reaching the local community with the Gospel; the mission is clear—helping people become more fully devoted followers of Jesus Christ. Pastor Jackson takes an active role in leading a variety of World Outreach Church community events that provide opportunities for families to experience God.

Pastor Jackson spearheaded the Mighty Men Conference U.S.A. featuring Angus Buchan. It was the first of its kind with over 10,000 men in attendance. This year, a second conference is expected to double attendance numbers and beyond.

From the humble beginnings in rural Tennessee, Pastor Jackson's messages now broadcast via television to over 25 million households including reaching over 90 million people in Russian speaking countries. In addition, his services stream over the Internet across five time zones and expand to over 139 countries.

The message of an extraordinary God using ordinary people has resonated with tens of thousands of households utilizing the home-based curriculum. The initial launch included home groups in 33 states outside of Tennessee and quickly expanded past borders from the US to Israel, Guatemala, Philippines, Bermuda, Mexico and South Africa. It certainly has been an extraordinary story.

Pastor Jackson earned a Bachelor of Arts from Oral Roberts University, a Master of Arts in Religious Studies from Vanderbilt University and studied at Hebrew University in Jerusalem. He has pursued additional studies at Gordon-Conwell Theological Seminary in Boston.

Pastor Jackson is often a featured speaker by the International Christian Embassy-Jerusalem Feast of Tabernacles celebration in Israel. He is recognized by the Christian Coalition of the Israeli Knesset for his continued support. Through Intend Ministries, Jackson coaches pastors across the nation and the world to greater effectiveness in their congregations. Pastor Jackson is married, and his wife, Kathy, is an active participant in ministry at World Outreach Church.

Your Extraordinary Life
Choosing God's Best For Your Life

SIX WEEK VIDEO STUDY

Discover how to live an Extraordinary Life. Think of it this way: the ordinary life is the life anyone could lead; the extraordinary life is the only life you can lead. Because there's no one else like you!

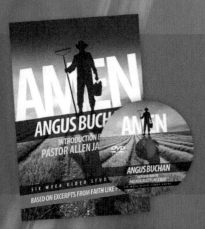

AMEN
SIX WEEK VIDEO STUDY

This six week DVD driven study will help you to personalize your own God story and turn His invitations into practical applicaton. Each session contains an introduction from Pastor Allen Jackson, a clip from the movie Faith Like Potatoes and a teaching session from Angus Buchan.

Freedom From Worry
(STUDY GUIDE & DVD)

Contains one six-session study DVD from Pastor Allen Jackson and one Study Guide.

Through these 6 sessions, your group can learn to overcome anxiety with God's love, purpose and power. To move beyond worry is to press into life with a renewed vision of who God is, and with a recognition of His strength and provision in our lives.

Join us for our
ISRAEL TOUR
wochurch.org/tour | (615) 896-4515

ANNUAL SUMMER TOUR
Join Pastor Allen on an immersive journey to the Holy
Land to see first-hand the places that set the stage for so
much of our Bible. To learn more and see for yourself,
check out wochurch.org/tour or call (615) 896-4515.

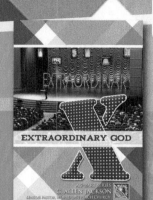

INTEND MINISTRIES was launched to take the transforming message of God's Word to where people live—through radio and television broadcasts, web streaming, podcasting, books and other media tools. Helping people become more fully devoted followers of Jesus Christ is at the heart of Intend Ministries. Church leaders who want to make a difference and experience growth in their congregations are given practical tools for effectiveness, proven strategies for taking the "next step" in their ministry, and help in breaking the barriers of growth that every church faces. Intend Ministries has conducted seminars and training for church pastors and leaders, focusing on growth, leadership, creating and maintaining momentum, and vision casting.

CPSIA information can be obtained at www.ICGtesting.com
Printed in the USA
LVOW01s1258160913

352647LV00001B/1/P